What Does It Mean
That God Is Sovereign?

Crucial Questions booklets provide a quick introduction to definitive Christian truths. This expanding collection includes titles such as:

Who Is Jesus?

Can I Trust the Bible?

Does Prayer Change Things?

Can I Know God's Will?

How Should I Live in This World?

What Does It Mean to Be Born Again?

Can I Be Sure I'm Saved?

What Is Faith?

What Can I Do with My Guilt?

What Is the Trinity?

TO BROWSE THE REST OF THE SERIES, PLEASE VISIT: LIGONIER.ORG/CQ

CQ

What Does It Mean It Mean That God Is Sovereign?

R.C. SPROUL

LIGONIER MINISTRIES

What Does It Mean That God Is Sovereign?
© 2021 by the R.C. Sproul Trust

Published by Ligonier Ministries
421 Ligonier Court, Sanford, FL 32771
Ligonier.org

Printed in China
RR Donnelley
0000122
First printing

ISBN 978-1-64289-335-9 (Paperback)
ISBN 978-1-64289-336-6 (ePub)
ISBN 978-1-64289-337-3 (Kindle)

Cover design: Ligonier Creative
Interior typeset: Katherine Lloyd, The DESK

Scripture quotations are from the ESV® Bible (The Holy Bible, English Standard Version®), copyright © 2001 by Crossway, a publishing ministry of Good News Publishers. Used by permission. All rights reserved.

Library of Congress Control Number: 2021931235

Contents

Chapter One

God's Sovereignty over Nothing

The title of this opening chapter might cause confusion. God's sovereignty over nothing? Doesn't that suggest that there is nothing over which God is sovereign? But surely God's sovereignty extends over everything. To find out what we mean by "God's sovereignty over nothing," we must go back to the beginning, to Genesis 1:

> In the beginning, God created the heavens and the earth. The earth was without form and void, and

darkness was over the face of the deep. And the Spirit of God was hovering over the face of the waters.

And God said, "Let there be light," and there was light. And God saw that the light was good. And God separated the light from the darkness. God called the light Day, and the darkness he called Night. And there was evening and there was morning, the first day.

And God said, "Let there be an expanse in the midst of the waters, and let it separate the waters from the waters." And God made the expanse and separated the waters that were under the expanse from the waters that were above the expanse. And it was so. (Gen. 1:1–7)

And so the text of Genesis continues, day by day, segment by segment, expressing the transcendent mystery of all mysteries: the creation of all things by a sovereign God. Augustine of Hippo described this as a work accomplished *ex nihilo*, out of nothing.

It might be easy for us to say that God creates *ex nihilo*, but to conceive of this work of creation is beyond our intellectual capacity. The first element, the idea of nothing, is beyond our ability to comprehend. What is nothing?

It's nothing. The problem with nothing is that when we say, "There is nothing," we are speaking nonsense because the verb *is* is a form of the verb *to be*, and the one thing that nothingness lacks is "*be*-ness." So, we can't speak of nothingness, and we can't say, "There is nothing" or "There was nothing," because to say that there *is* such a thing as nothing would be to attribute something to it, when *nothing is not*.

When we speak of *nothing*, we are using a word that functions as a type of definition that has a rich history in theological and philosophical investigation: the way of negation. The way of negation is a method of definition by which we define something not by stating positively what it *is* but rather by using negative language to say what it is *not*.

In theology, we use the way of negation all the time. When we say, for example, that God is infinite, what are we saying? He's not finite. When we say that God is immutable, we are saying that He is not given to change and mutation.

When we talk about *nothing*, we are using the way of negation and making a distinction between *something* and its negation. And the negation of *something* is *nothing*, or the *absence* of something is what we mean by nothing. The absence of what? If it's an ontological negation, that means that nothing would be the absence or lack of being.

There isn't anything that expresses more dramatically the holiness and majesty of God than the idea that God is sovereign over nothing, because it means that God in His greatness alone has the capacity of being within Himself, in and of Himself eternally, independently, without any assistance from matter, energy, or anything outside Himself.

Try to do what dreaming rocks try to do. Try to think of nothing abstractly. Think that there was a time in the past when nothing existed, absolute nothingness, where all that was (even *was* is a misnomer) was shrouded in darkness. The universe was a pure vacuum, completely empty and void of any reality. There was nothing, absolute nothingness.

If there ever was such a time where nothing was, absolute nothingness, what would there be today? Nothing. Because the one absolute axiom of logic and of science is the principle *ex nihilo nihil fit*—"out of nothing, nothing comes." And if there ever was a time when there was absolutely nothing, then nothingness would reign supreme.

Nothingness would be immutably nothingness, sovereignly nothingness. And there would be no possibility of anything's existing.

I don't believe that we can give just probable evidence for the existence of God. I believe that the existence of God can be demonstrated conclusively and irrefutably on the basis of reason alone. If you grant one thing, that something exists—a piece of chalk, a shoe—then something must *be*. There must be something somewhere, somehow that has the power of being itself, something that you and I don't have. If anything exists, then something, somewhere, somehow must have what Thomas Aquinas called "necessary being," which means the power of being that is not dependent or derived but is located within oneself. And if it is essential and intrinsic to something to *be*, then that being must be an eternal being.

"In the beginning." Eternity has no beginning. Genesis begins with a statement about the beginning not of eternity but of time, the beginning not of God but of the created realm. Why? Because there is no beginning to God. There is no beginning to eternity. But suppose there were a beginning to eternity. Suppose there were a beginning to God. What would there have been before God? Nothing.

And we would be talking about the sovereignty of nothingness (if we could be talking about anything). But we
wouldn't be talking about the sovereignty of nothingness
because there wouldn't be any of us here to be able to talk.
Because if there ever were a time when there was nothing,
what would there be now? Nothing.

So to talk about the beginning of anything, there must
first be something that eternally transcends nothingness,
that which eternally is in the beginning—God.

Now, I have no interest in indulging in intellectual
speculation for the sake of playing around with abstrac-
tions. We are talking about the very essence of Christian
faith. The question of creation is one of the most con-
troversial topics of our day. And it is not something that
Christians can afford to take for granted. People can argue
all they want about how long creation took and what was
the mode of creation, but the fundamental issue today is
creation at all.

A host of educated people tell us that, in fact, there was a
time when there was nothing and then . . . poof! Suddenly,
there was something. This is intellectual madness. And yet
somehow it has gained respectability. Equally absurd is
the idea that all available energy was compressed into one

infinitesimal point of singularity and stayed in a steady state of inertia for eternity and then suddenly, without any outside force, this inert mass of something blew up.

The Apostle Paul addressed the philosophers at Mars Hill by saying that what the Bible teaches in Hebrew on the first page of the Old Testament, nature screams aloud, and they should understand as even the pagan philosophers did that "in him we live and move and have our being" (Acts 17:28).

In the ancient world, philosophers had to deal with three thorny questions. The first was the question of motion. Is motion real or is it an illusion? Zeno of Elea argued against the reality of material objects because, as he said, if matter exists, then matter must be endlessly divisible. That is, I can take a piece of chalk and break it in half and then have two pieces. Now, presumably, we could break each piece in half, and we could do this again. How long could we do that? According to Zeno, we could do that forever.

He then applied this idea to motion. He told a story about Achilles and a turtle. Achilles was the champion Greek athlete, the fastest runner in all of creation. He was going to enter a race against a turtle. Since everybody recognized that the turtle didn't have the velocity or fleetness of foot that was intrinsic to Achilles, they decided to make the race a bit more fair by giving the turtle a head start. The race begins, and Achilles races to the point where the turtle is. But of course, before he can reach the turtle, he has to go halfway to the turtle, doesn't he? And then to bridge the gap between the halfway point to where the turtle is, he has to get halfway. Now, reasoning in this fashion, how long will it take Achilles to catch the turtle? He'll never catch the turtle.

The first big question that ancient philosophers asked was "What is motion?" The next two questions were "What is life?" and "What is being?" Those were the three great mysteries of antiquity. And here we are today, and we still don't know what is being, what is life, and what is motion. All we know is that these elements are essential to human existence, and we can't even talk about anything without some understanding of, or reaction to, motion, life, and being.

While the philosophers were debating these things, Paul told them that there is One who is eternal, whose power is so powerful, whose sovereignty is so great that He transcends being, motion, and life, because apart from Him nothing can be, and apart from Him nothing can move. A point of singularity that was around for eternity would never explode. It would remain eternally inert unless acted on by an outside force that has the capacity of movement. Something must have the ability to move within itself. Something must have life within itself. Something must have the power of being within itself, or quite simply, nothing could move, nothing could live, nothing could be.

There might be times when you doubt the sovereignty of God or His very existence. At times you might feel, as Friedrich Nietzsche did, that the final answer to all reality is the nothingness, the *nihil*. If you're ever tempted to think that nothing is victorious over being, just wiggle your finger. Remember that. Anytime you doubt your destiny as a Christian, anytime you doubt the triumph of a sovereign God over the threat of chaos, the void, and the emptiness and darkness described in Genesis 1, wiggle your finger.

What is that going to remind you of? Motion, life, being. You could not wiggle your finger if there were no source of motion, if there were no source of life, if there were no source of being. If you can wiggle your finger, then God is sovereign. It's that simple, because without sovereign being, there is no being. Without sovereign being, there is no life. And without sovereign being, nothing can move. Simple and profound.

Some Old Testament scholars like to point out that ideas from Genesis 1 also appear in primitive mythology. The Babylonian myths, for example, talk about a primordial, dualistic struggle between the forces of order and the forces of chaos. But what we see in Genesis 1 and throughout the Old Testament is not an eternal standoff between equal and opposite forces that are locked in a perpetual contest but the triumph of the eternal God over every conceivable threat. In this prestructured, preordered, presaturated creation that God is bringing into existence, the Spirit of God begins to brood over the primordial waters, over the deep. We encounter the same image when God the Holy Spirit speaks to Mary through the angel: The Spirit of the Lord will come upon you, and the power of the Almighty will *overshadow* you so that that which is conceived in your womb will be called the Son of God (see Luke 1:35).

It's the same language. It's the language of the transcendent power of God hovering over the darkness and the emptiness and the abyss, over the nothingness. And He says, "Let there be light." The divine fiat is uttered. The divine imperative is spoken, and by the power of the Almighty's

Word, the lights come on and the ocean begins to teem with life, and motion and being fill the universe because of this great God in heaven who has the power of being within Himself and who alone has the ability to call worlds out of nothing, to bring life out of death, motion out of inertia, being out of nothingness.

Just looking at creation should drive us to our knees. In creation we see reflected unspeakable, ineffable majesty, sovereignty, dominion, power, and glory. That's our God, without whom we can't wiggle a finger. But because we can wiggle our finger, we know the God of heaven.

Chapter Two

God's Sovereignty over Creation

Five times in Isaiah 45, and considerably more often throughout the whole book of Isaiah, God speaks emphatically the words "I am the LORD" or "I, the LORD."

> "I will give you the treasures of darkness
>   and the hoards in secret places,
> that you may know that it is I, the LORD,
>   the God of Israel, who call you by your name.
> For the sake of my servant Jacob,
>   and Israel my chosen,

I call you by your name,
    I name you, though you do not know me.
I am the LORD, and there is no other,
    besides me there is no God;
    I equip you, though you do not know me,
that people may know, from the rising of the sun
        and from the west, that there is none besides me;
    I am the LORD, and there is no other.
I form light and create darkness;
    I make well-being and create calamity;
    I am the LORD, who does all these things.

"Shower, O heavens, from above,
    and let the clouds rain down righteousness;
let the earth open, that salvation and righteousness
        may bear fruit;
    let the earth cause them both to sprout;
    I the LORD have created it.

"Woe to him who strives with him who formed him,
    a pot among earthen pots!
Does the clay say to him who forms it, 'What are
        you making?'

or 'Your work has no handles'?
Woe to him who says to a father, 'What are you
    begetting?'
    or to a woman, 'With what are you in labor?'"

Thus says the LORD,
    the Holy One of Israel, and the one who
    formed him:
"Ask me of things to come;
    will you command me concerning my children
and the work of my hands?" (vv. 3–11)

When the Hubble Space Telescope was launched into
outer space, scientists were excited about the possibility of
gathering a huge surplus of new data that would give insight
to the dawn of creation and to the machinations involved
in the solar system and beyond. On the day of the launch,
I listened to one of the most celebrated astrophysicists in
America declare that sixteen to eighteen billion years ago
the universe exploded into being. I said, to nobody in particular, "Sixteen to eighteen billion years ago the universe
exploded into being? I thought you were a scientist, not a
practitioner of magic who sees the universe as something

that arises as a rabbit out of the hat, only without the hat and without the magician."

If there is any immutable law of secular science, it is that law that declares *ex nihilo nihil fit*, "out of nothing, nothing comes." And the reason for that law is that something does not come from nothing simply because it cannot come from nothing. If there had ever been a time when there was absolutely nothing—no being, no thing—what could there possibly be now?

Unless you argue that things pop into being from nothing, then the only answer is that there would be nothing now. The oldest philosophical question is, Why is there something rather than nothing?

You don't have to be a rocket scientist to understand that if anything exists right now, then there could never have been a time when nothing existed. Even if it were sixteen to eighteen billion years ago, there had to be some being, or else nothing today could be.

The Bible makes it clear what that eternal self-existent being is: the Lord God, who creates all things. "I am the LORD," He says, "and there is no other, besides me there is no God" (v. 5).

Fallen humanity knows that if we can do away with the

Christian doctrine of creation, if we can do away with the very first verse of the Old Testament, then we can destroy Judeo-Christianity at its root and enjoy the freedom of doing anything we want to do. The attack on creation is fallen man's attempt at a declaration of independence from the Creator.

Why? Because the biblical Creator has little resemblance to Aristotle's concept of the first cause or the unmoved mover. Modern philosophers often say that the whole history of theoretical thought is merely a footnote to the speculations of Plato and Aristotle. Aristotle understood as an early scientist that there had to be some uncaused cause to explain the presence of reality. That prime mover, that uncaused cause, was given the role of creator, but after his work of creation he had nothing further to do with the universe.

In stark contrast to that is the biblical teaching that whatever God creates, He sustains. And not only do we owe God as Creator our own origin of human existence, but we also owe our Creator our moment-to-moment existence. That is to say, we cannot exist for the next five seconds without the sustaining power of God.

What God creates, He sustains and upholds by the power of His might. We understand that we can do nothing apart from the sustaining power of God, as the Apostle Paul said to the Athenians on Mars Hill: "In him we live and move and have our being" (Acts 17:28).

If God is out of the picture, so is life. If God disappears, so does all motion. And if God should die, all being disappears with Him. Whatever God creates, He sustains. Whatever He creates, He owns, and whatever He owns, He rules. He rules over all things.

Sometimes Christians get confused about predestination and free will, as if they are opposites. We must understand that free will is not simply a pagan concept, though the pagan conception enjoys widespread approval. Christians also believe in free will, but the free will that we believe in is not the humanistic or pagan version of it. One secular idea that has been pervasive in the church today is the humanistic doctrine of human freedom that says that our will, even in our fallen condition, remains indifferent and equally able to incline ourselves to the good or to the evil. It ignores the biblical revelation that though we have the power of choosing, our choices are in bondage to sin. Only the power of God the Holy Spirit can rescue us from that bondage, that spiritual death, and that paralysis.

We have to get our view of the human will not from

the secular culture but from the Word of God. Not only are we deficient at that point, but also the pagan world has intruded into our thinking the idea that this world functions according to internal independent laws of nature and of physics.

The idea is that the universe operates moment to moment under its own steam without the transcendent sovereign power of God enabling it and ordaining it. I cannot lift my arm, for example, apart from the power of God. Whatever power I have in my right arm to exercise my will is at best secondary in its causal expression, but all the things that I do in this world are done under and because of the transcendent sovereign power of God.

Some say God is sovereign, but God's sovereignty is limited by human freedom. If that were the case, then who is sovereign? We have been given a measure of freedom by our Creator, but our freedom is always and everywhere limited by God's freedom. God is sovereign, not we ourselves, and His sovereignty extends to all things, not only the creation of the world but the sustaining and governing of the world, and what we describe as the laws of nature only describe the ordinary ways that God in His sovereignty governs nature.

If there is one maverick molecule in this universe running free from the sovereign control of God, we have no reason to believe any future promise that God has made, because that one maverick molecule may be the very thing that will destroy those plans. But thanks be to God, there are no maverick molecules running loose outside of the scope of God's sovereign government.

I once was asked to teach a seminary course on the theology of the Westminster Confession of Faith. When we got to the section of the confession on the eternal decrees of God, the seminary students brought their non-Reformed friends to the class. And to this group of inquisitive seminarians I read, with no explanation, the first section of this part of the confession: "God from all eternity did . . . freely, and unchangeably ordain whatsoever comes to pass" (WCF 3.1). I then asked: "How many of you believe that? How many believe that God immutably and eternally ordains every single thing that comes to pass?"

Now, I was in a Reformed seminary. So it wasn't astonishing that 175 students raised their hands. In any other general seminary, that would have been astonishing. But about seventy-five students didn't raise their hands.

I then asked, "How many of you would describe yourselves as atheists?" No students raised their hands. I said: "There's just one thing I don't understand. You didn't affirm that God ordains whatsoever comes to pass. And yet, you didn't say that you are an atheist. But if God doesn't ordain everything that comes to pass, then God isn't sovereign. And if God isn't sovereign, then God is not God."

We then examined more carefully what the confession really means. It goes on to say that secondary causes are not eliminated; nor is violence done to the will of man. God is not the author or doer of sin. Centuries earlier, Augustine said that as Christians who believe in a sovereign God, we have to affirm that, in some sense, God must ordain whatsoever comes to pass.

Some people are quick to bring up the concept of God's "permissive will." This concept has been invented as a way to excuse God from responsibility for those things we don't want to assign to Him. But God knows what's going to happen before it happens. He knows what I am going to say before I say it. He knows what I am going to do before I do it. Does God have the power to stop me? Does God have the right to stop me if He so chooses? If He permits me to commit a sin, He has chosen to permit me. If He chooses to permit it, He deems it wise that it should come to pass, or else He would not permit it because He does all things well, including the exercise of His sovereignty.

In Genesis 37 we read about Joseph's brothers, who were guilty and responsible for the sins they committed against their brother, the betrayal and treachery that sent him to languish in prison, removed from his family. Later Joseph said, "You meant evil against me, but God meant it for good" (Gen. 50:20).

Now, the Bible says we are never to call evil good or good evil (Isa. 5:20). Evil is evil, and evil is deserving of divine retribution. But it is good that there is evil, or evil could not be, because all things are under the scope of God's sovereignty, including our wickedness, which He uses for His righteous purposes. That God can be involved in catastrophic events or in the evil actions of fallen human beings becomes a matter of national interest when catastrophic events such as hurricanes and tsunamis occur. People say, "This is an accident of nature." But even the insurance companies have enough sense to call these things "acts of God." When we go beyond natural calamities and look at calamities foisted on us by human wickedness, we find it all the more difficult to think that God's sovereignty could somehow be behind it.

After 9/11, some Christian leaders opined that the attacks were God's judgment on the rampant immorality of our culture. Those observations outraged the press, who demanded that the men retract their comments. It was an unthinkable idea to the American public that God could possibly be involved in such a calamity, because apparently they never read Isaiah 45: "I am the LORD, and there is no other, besides me there is no God; . . . I am the LORD, and there is no other. I form light and create darkness; I make well-being and I create calamity; I am the LORD, who does all these things" (Isa. 45:5–7).

Two things happened out of 9/11. First, there was a fresh awakening in the public consciousness about the reality of evil. All of a sudden, moral relativism was arrested as people witnessed an event that they could not regard as morally indifferent but that must be viewed as unspeakably wicked. There was a new acceptance of the idea of sin. Second, there came a revival of interest of God's blessing a given nation. All over the country—on windows, bumpers, and everywhere else—was the slogan "God bless America."

Now, the same people who were praying for God to bless America were the people who thought it completely impossible that God could judge America. If you pray that God would bless a nation, certainly in your prayer you must allow for the possibility that He might not, that indeed, if He's capable of bringing prosperity and peace to a nation, then He must also be capable of withdrawing that blessing and even bringing calamity and wrath on it.

But our understanding of God has degenerated into a cosmic bellhop, a celestial Santa Claus, who exists to serve our needs and to give us nice things when we inquire after Him, but we will not bow before His sovereignty that extends over all things.

I generally say that there are four ways that God is sovereign. He is sovereign over nature. He is sovereign over history and human affairs. And He is sovereign in His inherent right to impose obligations on His creatures, to say to them, "Thou shalt not do this" and "Thou shalt do that." Do we believe that He has that sovereignty, that right to command obedience from us and impose obligations on us?

Every time we sin, we challenge God's sovereign right to command what we should do. Some Christians believe that God is sovereign over nature and history and morality but not over His grace. They deny that He has the eternal inherent right to give His mercy to whom He will give mercy.

I'll conclude with Romans 11:36: "For from him and through him and to him are all things. To him be glory forever. Amen." *From* Him: He is the source, the author of all that is good, true, beautiful, and real. *Through* Him: by means of His sovereign power and agency. Not only do all things come from Him, but they come by means of His power. *To* Him: the purpose for all things is not me. It is not you. It is Him. All things are from Him, through Him, and to Him, or we could say *for* Him. And it ends with a doxology: "To Him be glory forever." *Soli Deo gloria*, to God alone the glory.

Every time we discount the scope of the sovereignty of God over all things, we rob Him of His glory.

Chapter Three

God's Sovereignty over Salvation

When Augustine of Hippo came to the end of his life, he wrote a little-known work called *Retractationes*, or *The Retractions*. A retraction is what you find in the back page of the daily newspaper or your monthly magazine that admits to certain errors that were committed in a previous publication. These retractions are normally buried where few people will see them because it seems to be an embarrassment for us to admit mistakes.

Augustine, however, was open about the publication of his retractions. By the time he reached his later years, he had reflected on what he had spoken earlier, and he realized that some things he had written earlier were not necessarily precise.

Now, I know I've already reached the point where it's long overdue to publish some retraction. Here I want to make one significant theological retraction.

When I became a Christian in 1957 as a freshman in college, I was assigned to a particular professor who would be my faculty advisor. This professor was a Calvinist. He not only had his doctor's degree in philosophy from the University of Pennsylvania, but he also had a master's degree from Westminster Theological Seminary. For four years, like the hound of heaven, he relentlessly sought to persuade me of the Reformed faith and the truths of Calvinistic thinking. But I resisted tenaciously and graduated from college after my first four years of Christian conviction still strongly and adamantly committed to semi-Pelagianism. I managed to resist the arguments of Dr. John Gerstner in seminary for at least a year and make it through five years of my Christian walk without acquiescing to the biblical doctrine of predestination.

And then, after reading Jonathan Edwards' *Freedom of the Will* and being forced to deal with the topic of sovereignty in an in-depth manner, and following the advice I had written to myself on a card that I posted over my desk as a seminary student—"You are required to believe, to affirm, to teach, and to preach everything the Bible teaches, not what you want the Bible to teach"—I finally surrendered and acquiesced to the sovereignty of God in all its fullness.

Initially, murmuring and grumbling like the Israelites, I reluctantly accepted the doctrine of predestination. I said, "OK, the Bible teaches it." I didn't add the dreadful mediating line that we hear in modern evangelicalism: "The Bible says it. I believe it. That settles it." Rather, once I understood that the Bible taught it, it didn't matter whether I believed it; the issue was settled. The truth of God never depends on my submission to it for its truthfulness.

God has a sense of humor and is committed to a particular kind of poetic justice. He made me a teacher of Calvinism to a world that was fiercely resistant, even to the degree that I had resisted it. And because I had resisted it so vehemently and for so long, I had to say every time

I encountered a person who was kicking and screaming against the biblical doctrine of election: "R.C., you must be patient, because after all, you stood where that person stood and you fought it as vigorously as you knew how. How can you in any way be judgmental toward another person who struggles desperately against the doctrine of predestination?"

And so, to exhibit a sense of patience and compassion with dear friends who struggled deeply with the doctrine of predestination, trying as hard as I knew how to be sensitive, I would preface my remarks by saying: "How difficult, complex, and mysterious is this doctrine of predestination. It is a doctrine that we must treat with the greatest of care and caution and be careful that we don't wound or injure people by an insensitive approach to it." I would go on and on about how difficult it is to gain a clear understanding of this doctrine. It is that technique and that tactic that I now repent of and retract. Recently I was reading Calvin's careful exegesis of John 6 and Romans 9, where he made the casual observation, as Augustine did, that this doctrine of predestination is taught in sacred Scripture. And it suddenly hit me that all these years I have been telling people it's somewhat difficult to perceive in Scripture and that I understand the struggle we have with the doctrine.

All that time I didn't realize that as I was trying so hard to be nice to people, I was slandering the Holy Spirit. I was accusing God of being muddled, of being less than clear in this doctrine that Martin Luther called the *cor ecclesiae*, "the heart of the church." As I went back to those texts, I said to myself: "How could John, repeating for us the teaching of our Lord Himself, possibly have stated any more clearly the utter dependence of a fallen human being on the prior work of the sovereign grace of God to bring us to faith? How could the doctrine of unconditional election be stated more plainly, more simply, or more convincingly than the Apostle Paul did in Romans 9?"

When we talk about the sovereignty of God, what are we talking about? We do not mean simply that God is boss, that God rules by His transcendent authority. Rather, we must speak of different facets or aspects when we talk about divine sovereignty.

The first thing we have in view when we're talking about sovereignty is the *power* of God. When we say that God is sovereign, we are saying that His power is supreme in all reality, and no power in heaven or on earth can possibly resist the power of God. If there is a conflict between His power and lesser powers, the outcome is not in dispute. God's power is ultimate. His power is sovereign.

Second, we reference His *authority*, His intrinsic and inherent right to impose obligations on His creatures, to bind our consciences, to proclaim our duty by saying to us, "Thou shalt not do this or thou shalt do that." God has sovereign authority over me. If there is a conflict between what I want and what God commands, where does the authority reside? We don't have to debate that among Christians. God possesses sovereign authority, and that authority in no way rests on my agreement or submission to it.

We believe that God is sovereign in His *power*. We believe that God is sovereign in His *authority*. But here is where the disembarkation point rests. Is God sovereign in His *grace*? Does God determine from the foundation of the world who will be redeemed, or does the determining factor of our salvation rest with us rather than with Him?

Ultimately, is salvation of the Lord or is it of man? Is it of His grace, sovereignly distributed, or is it by the exercise of our human will? Pelagianism and humanism have always insisted that the decisive critical point is in the will of man. That is simply not Christian. That is an affront against the sovereignty of God's grace. And today, the church is being held in a death grip by the ancient Pelagian heresy that casts an eclipsing shadow over the brightness of the glory of God's sovereign grace.

If you do not believe in the sovereignty of grace, I plead with you to repent and to come home to the God who by His sheer mercy, without any view to any righteousness, merit, or willingness on your part, has from the foundation of the world, entirely by His grace and solely according to the good pleasure of His will, chosen you as His gift to His only begotten Son.

One of the most important books ever written in Christendom is Martin Luther's *The Bondage of the Will*. It is a delight to read. It's brilliant; it's lucid; it's penetrating. We know that at the center of the Reformation was the dispute over the question "How is an unjust person made just in the sight of God?" How are we saved? This was not a tangential issue. It was not much ado about nothing. Luther was right when he said the issue of justification was the article on which the church stands or falls. It's the article on which you stand or fall.

Closely connected to the controversy over justification by faith alone is *sola gratia*, justification by grace alone.

The principle of *sola fide* is never rightly understood until it is seen as anchored in the broader principle of *sola gratia*. What is the source and status of faith? Where does faith come from? Is faith the God-given means whereby the God-given justification is received, or is it a *condition* of justification that is left to man to fulfill? Is faith a part of God's gift of salvation, or is it man's own contribution to salvation? Is our salvation wholly of God, or does it ultimately depend on something that we do for ourselves?

Those who say the latter, as Arminians did (and still do), deny man's utter helplessness in sin and affirm that a form of semi-Pelagianism is true after all. It is no wonder that later Reformed theology condemned Arminianism as being, in principle, a return to Rome. In effect, it turned faith into a meritorious work and was a betrayal of the Reformation because it denied the sovereignty of God in saving sinners, which was the deepest religious and theological principle of the Reformers' thought. Arminian theology, which is the overwhelming majority report among evangelicals today, stands opposed to the sovereignty of God and to the primacy of grace.

The Apostle John wrote: "Jesus said to them, 'I am the bread of life; whoever comes to me shall not hunger, and whoever believes in me shall never thirst. But I said to you that you have seen me and yet do not believe'" (John 6:35–36). This isn't Calvin. This isn't Luther. This isn't Augustine. This isn't Edwards. This is Jesus. "All that the Father gives me will come to me, and whoever comes to me I will never cast out" (v. 37).

Beloved, Jesus did not say, "All who will come to Me, My Father will give to Me." Our Lord says that all whom the Father gives to the Son come to the Son. Every one of them. Every person whom God the Father gives to God the Son comes to faith in the Son. And the reason they come to faith in the Son is because God the Father brings them to faith in the Son.

You know Arminians and semi-Pelagians can't get away from predestination because it's a biblical word. It's a biblical concept. It's right there in the New Testament. If you are going to be biblical, you have to have some doctrine of predestination, don't you? So, the question is, What is the correct doctrine?

The standard semi-Pelagian view is that God looks down the corridor of time from all eternity, and He knows who will in the future say yes to the invitation of the gospel of Jesus Christ and who will say no. On the basis of this prescience or foreknowledge, God elects those who He knows will say yes to the gospel to be His children, and He rejects those who He knows in advance will say no.

This is really not an explanation of predestination. It is the denial of biblical predestination. Scripture's view is that if God looks down the corridor of time at fallen human beings who are dead in sin and trespasses, unregenerate, and in bondage to sin to see which ones are going to incline, direct, and move themselves toward the living God, how many people will God notice doing that? None.

If God's election is based on God's foreknowledge of human actions, and we know that God's foreknowledge is perfect, then we know the number of the elect: zero. Because all God sees when He looks down the corridor of time is people who are dead in sin and trespasses, who are by nature at enmity with God, who refuse to even have God in their thoughts, who have no inclination in their stony hearts whatsoever to come to Christ, and who are morally unable to come to Christ unless God intervenes.

But what about free will? Don't people have the moral ability to choose? Do people have the power to choose what they want while they are dead in sin and trespasses?

Of course they do. If all we mean by free will is man's ability to make choices according to what he wants, then yes, we still have free will even though we're spiritually dead. In fact, the problem with our spiritual death is not that we don't have free will; it's that our will is most free indeed to do whatever we want to do. And what we want is to flee as fast as we can from anything that has to do with the living Christ, because we are free to choose what we want and we are not free to choose what we don't want. And what we don't want naturally is God.

But what if I say that I have the moral power, unaided by regeneration and before I am born again, to incline myself to the things of God through an act of my flesh? Do I have that kind of free will? Absolutely not. That's an ability we don't have.

When I was studying the doctrine of predestination, I struggled as I read Romans 9:13: "Jacob I loved, but Esau I hated." Paul is teaching that before Jacob and Esau were born, before they had done any good or evil, the purposes of election according to the counsel of God stood firm. Paul goes on to say, "So then it depends not on human will or exertion, but on God, who has mercy" (v. 16). I was trying to hold on to my will and my choice; God did 99 percent, but Sproul hung on to that 1 percent. And that decisive 1 percent got me into the kingdom rather than into hell and persuaded and induced God from all eternity to elect me.

I was devastated by the power of the Word of God, and I realized my utter helplessness in my spiritual death. And I kept coming back to John 6 and linking it with Romans 9. I hear Paul ask, "Is there injustice on God's part?" (Rom. 9:14). Paul answers by repeating what Moses had proclaimed to the people of God in the Old Testament: "I will have mercy upon whom I have mercy" (v. 15). We don't like that. We say: "Wait a minute, God. If You have mercy on one person, You must have mercy on everyone."

Why does Paul ask, "Is there injustice on God's part?" That's what hit me in my studies. If Paul were teaching a semi-Pelagian view of salvation here, why would he anticipate an objection that there is unrighteousness in God?

The whole system of Pelagianism is designed to answer any possible charge of unrighteousness in God. Even some of Jesus' own disciples didn't like what Jesus said about election and divine sovereignty, and many left Him (John

6:60–66). Then Jesus asked the Twelve, "Do you want to go away as well?" (v. 67). And what did Peter say? Did he say, "Oh no, I love the doctrines of grace; they affirm my flesh so much"? No. Peter said: "Lord, to whom shall we go? You have the words of eternal life" (v. 68). You see, in John 6 after Jesus said that all whom the Father gives to Him come to Him (v. 37), He says something about natural human ability. He says, "No one can come to me unless the Father who sent me draws him" (v. 44), and then He repeated the same sentiment and changed one word: "No one can come to me unless it is granted him by the Father" (v. 65).

Semi-Pelagians think that in our fallen, unregenerate state we have it within us to come to Jesus Christ. But our Lord says, "You can't." And we didn't. He uses a universal negative proposition: "No one can." It's not "No one *may*." "Can" has to do with power, with ability. Nobody, Jesus is saying, has the ability in and of himself to come to Jesus unless a necessary condition is met. And that necessary condition is that the Father draws him.

When Arminians read "unless the Father draws him," they think God must woo, entice, set the bait, try to persuade, and try to win by being as pleasing as He possibly can. Nobody can come without that wooing. But the Arminian assumption is that if God externally entices people to come to Jesus, if He tries to persuade them of the sweetness of Christ, a certain percentage of them will respond positively to that wooing and say yes.

A better translation of the word for "draw" is "compel" or "drag." The same word is used to describe Paul and Silas' being cast into prison. The jailer did not try to persuade them to become locked up. They were dragged into the prison. They were compelled.

One Arminian New Testament scholar pointed out to me a usage in an obscure place in Greek literature where the same verb was used to take water out of a well. He said, "We don't drag water out of a well." I replied: "Well, how do we get water from a well? Do we woo water out of a well? Or is that water lifeless and inert? Is it as dead as your soul in its fallen condition, which will remain in that state of spiritual death unless the life of God is breathed into that soul, effectively awakening you and causing your heart that was a heart of stone now to beat and pulsate like a heart of flesh? Then the scales are removed from your eyes and you see the sweetness of Christ, and there's nothing you want more desperately than the vision of Christ after the Holy Spirit has made you alive."

Jesus said it another way: "No one can come to me unless it is granted him by the Father." The point that Jesus made in John's gospel and that Paul labored in Romans 9 and Ephesians 2 is that everyone to whom the Father gives the ability to come to Christ is also one that the Father is giving to Christ. And everyone to whom is given the gift of regeneration, who is called in the depths of his soul, is sovereignly brought to faith in Jesus Christ. Salvation is of the Lord. That's what the sovereignty of God is all about. We praise Him.

I ask my Arminian friends: "Why do you believe in Christ but your friends at home don't? Are you a believer because you're more righteous intrinsically than somebody who doesn't believe? Why do you have faith? Where does your faith come from? Does it come from your flesh? If it comes from the flesh, you can boast. You can stand before the judgment seat of God and say, 'The reason I'm standing before You is because of a decision I made.'"

Or we can say, "When I heard the gospel, I didn't even know that the secret, transcendent, sovereign, efficacious, supernatural, immediate power of Your Holy Spirit had invaded my soul and awakened me and made me alive to Jesus Christ. When the gospel was preached, I heard it through ears that were regenerate, I saw it through regenerate eyes, and I embraced it with a regenerate heart. I fairly ran to that altar to embrace my Savior. Yes, I chose Him, and I chose Him freely, but not until I had been resurrected from spiritual death by the sovereign supernatural power of the Holy Spirit."

The only reason I can find in Scripture that any of us has faith is that it is given according to the good pleasure of God's will. It pleased the Lord to rescue you from death, not because of any foreseen righteousness in you but according to the good pleasure of His will. And the only reason He did that was to honor His Son, to make Him the firstborn of many brethren and so that our Lord could see the travail of His soul and be satisfied. You are the gift of the Father to the Son, and the only merit that enters into this transaction is the merit of the Son, not yours and not mine.

Man's freedom is limited by God's sovereignty (not the other way around). God is free and you are free, but He is freer than you are, and when there's a conflict between His freedom and your freedom, guess which one wins? When we say to the world in all piety that God's sovereignty is limited by our freedom, we say that we are sovereign, and we are speaking blasphemy.

So if we really believe in the sovereignty of God, we will not only believe that God is sovereign in His power and in His authority, but we will also see that He is absolutely sovereign in His grace.

Chapter Four

God's Sovereignty over Human Actions

One of the most cold-blooded acts of treachery and betrayal occurs near the end of Genesis. Joseph, who was the apple of his father's eye, was sold into slavery by his jealous and envious brothers. They took his coat of many colors, dipped it in the blood of an animal, and made up a story for their father that, alas, Joseph had fallen prey to a ravenous beast and had been torn limb from limb and was no more. But in fact they had exploited their advantage and sold him to Ishmaelite caravanners and traders who were on their way to Egypt.

Many years later, through God's providence, Joseph had risen to the level of prime minister and embarked on a series of wise actions to see the nation through a prophesied famine. When the famine hit Canaan, Jacob sent his sons down to Egypt to get relief, to try to get goods from the storehouses to feed their family. They came to Pharaoh's court and were met there by Joseph. Joseph recognized them; they didn't recognize him. Eventually it became clear that the prime minister of Egypt was the brother whom they had betrayed.

Finally, we come to the end of the story where Jacob, after having learned that his son was still alive, has died, and the brothers now know that they don't have the protection of their father to shield them from the vengeful wrath of their brother. They are terrified, and they don't know how to deal with it.

When Joseph's brothers saw that their father was dead, they said, "It may be that Joseph will hate us and pay us back for all the evil that we did to him." So they sent a message to Joseph, saying,

"Your father gave this command before he died: 'Say to Joseph, "Please forgive the transgression of your brothers and their sin, because they did evil to you."' And now, please forgive the transgression of the servants of the God of your father." Joseph wept when they spoke to him. (Gen. 50:15–17)

The brothers recognized that Joseph had every right to hate them because what they had done to him was a despicable and hateful thing. They assumed that Joseph would seek revenge with the same kind of fury that they had exercised out of their jealousy and envy those many years before. So they begged for forgiveness, and they acknowledged that what they had done was evil. And Joseph wept in the midst of this acknowledgment of their sin, in the midst of their repentance. They confessed that what they did was wicked, and it brought the brother to tears.

Now, listen to what follows: "His brothers also came and fell down before him and said, 'Behold, we are your servants'" (v. 18). Doesn't that foreshadow the experience of the Prodigal Son in the New Testament, who, after living a life of licentiousness, came to himself and determined to return to his father's house? Coming in repentance, he said to his father, "Father, I have sinned against heaven and before you. I am no longer worthy to be called your son" (Luke 15:21). He essentially said: "I don't have to be a son. I just want to be in your house. And I'm happy to be there as your slave." Joseph's brothers similarly said: "We've wronged you. We don't expect you to receive us as your brothers. We are your servants."

How did Joseph respond? He said, "Do not fear, for am I in the place of God?" (Gen. 50:19). You're on your faces before me as if I were the living God. I'm just your brother. I'm not ruling in the place of God. "As for you, you meant evil against me" (v. 20). You acknowledge it. And I'm not going to sugarcoat it. What you did to me those years ago when you betrayed me and sold me into slavery was unspeakably wicked. It wasn't an accident. You knew exactly what you were doing. You meant it and intended it for evil.

It is as if Joseph were saying to his brothers: "I've thought about this a little bit over the last several decades. I had a lot of time in the prison to think about this, and I've had to deal with the possible root of bitterness that would grow up in my soul because of what you did to me, but I've come to understand that you were not the only players in this episode. I've come to understand that the sovereign God of the universe, the Lord God of Israel, was intimately involved in your wickedness. You couldn't have hurt me for a second. You couldn't have damaged my heart or destroyed my relationship with my father. You couldn't have had me delivered into the hands of my enemies and cast into prison for one second apart from the sovereign providence of God, because God's sovereignty was involved in your diabolical actions against me. I believe in a God who works all things together for good to those who love Him and who are called according to His purpose, and I believe that the Lord God of the universe has the sovereign power even to work your treachery against me for good."

The brothers could not say: "We were just carrying out the sovereign will of God. You can't be upset with us for that. We won't even say that the devil made us do it, but this sovereign God made us betray you." Joseph was not giving them that option. He clearly said that what they did was evil, and he did not call good evil or evil good. He told them that what they did, they meant for evil, but what they meant for evil, what they designed out of the wicked machinations of their hearts for evil, God meant for good. God's intent in all this was altogether righteous.

In His sovereignty, God has the capacity and ability to work through the sinful decisions and wicked choices of His creatures to bring about His sovereign will, which is altogether righteous.

The Apostle John has already shown how that works out in the New Testament, that the cross was not an accident. The cross was the most wicked evil ever perpetrated by human beings. Caiaphas meant it for evil. Pilate meant it for evil. The Pharisees meant it for evil. But over and above the human intentionality, the human decisions that grew out of the evil inclinations and impulses of fallen human beings, God was at work to bring about good.

In Genesis 50:20–21, Joseph said: "'As for you, you meant evil against me, but God meant it for good, to bring it about that many people should be kept alive, as they are today. So do not fear; I will provide for you and your little ones.' Thus he comforted them and spoke kindly to them"—not because of their good intentions, but because of God's good intention.

The old adage says: "For want of a nail, the shoe was lost. For want of the shoe, the horse was lost. For want of the horse, the rider was lost. For want of the rider, the message was lost. For want of the message, the battle was lost." The pivotal moment that decided the outcome of the battle was a single nail from the shoe of the horse. An insignificant detail became the pivotal reason for the loss of the battle. Have you ever wondered what led to the atonement of Christ on the cross, what led to your salvation? Just go back a little bit in time.

It all starts with a coat of many colors. If it weren't for that coat, Joseph's brothers would not have been jealous of him. No jealousy, no betrayal. No betrayal, no sale into slavery. No trip to Egypt, no Potiphar, no Potiphar's wife. No Potiphar's wife, no prison sentence. No prison sentence, no meeting the chief baker and chief cupbearer. If Joseph had never met them, he would never have been acquainted with Pharaoh. He would never have been elevated to prime minister. The children of Israel would not have settled in the land of Goshen. They would not have been enslaved. There would not have been an exodus. There would not have been a nation. There would not have been the Ten Commandments. There would not be a kingdom of God. "You meant evil against me, but God meant it for good," to save many people. That is incredible.

As Christians, we often struggle with the question, How do we reconcile the sovereignty of God with human freedom? When I was a new Christian, I was troubled by this question. I thought I was facing a contradiction between human freedom and divine sovereignty. I thought that if God is really sovereign, then we can't really be free, or if we're really free, then God can't really be sovereign.

While taking introduction to the Old Testament in college, I asked my professor to help me with this question. He said that God's sovereignty and human freedom are like parallel lines that meet in eternity. At the time, I thought that was profound, and my professor was really smart.

Later I was thinking about the professor's answer. "Parallel lines that meet in eternity," I pondered. "If those parallel lines meet in eternity—or if they meet in Albuquerque, in Dallas, in Atlanta, or New York City—then they're not really parallel lines, are they? Because if they're really parallel lines, they're not going to meet."

I began to realize that this is really not a tough question at all. It's a very simple question, with no contradiction. There is no real mystery. We have God, who is a being, and we have people, who are beings, and when we talk about the difference between the two, we call the people "human beings," and we call God the "supreme Being."

What is the relationship between human beings and

supreme beings? Only one is supreme. We don't call people "supreme beings"; we call them "human beings." It's God who is the supreme Being. Now, God is a volitional being. That is, God has a will. He has a divine faculty by which He makes decisions and choices. We, as His creatures, are also volitional beings, and part of our humanity is that our Creator has endowed us with the faculty of choosing, which we call *the will*. We have the ability to make choices. And that's what we're concerned about when we talk about freedom and free will: the ability to make choices.

Edmund Husserl was an important European philosopher in the nineteenth century. He was a founder of a school of philosophy called personalism, which tried to answer these questions: What makes human beings unique? What defines our existence as human beings, as persons? What does it mean to be a person rather than a thing? Husserl's answer was that human beings have the ability to act with intentionality. That is, we can conceive of a purpose that we want to accomplish, and we can make choices and decisions for the purpose of bringing that idea to pass. Husserl insisted that central to our humanness is the fact that we have the ability to make choices.

Two of Husserl's most famous students were Jean-Paul Sartre and Martin Heidegger. Sartre and Heidegger were two of the most significant atheistic philosophers of the twentieth century, and both were preoccupied with the concept of human volition. Sartre concluded that human freedom is the strongest argument there is against the existence of God. Sartre reasoned that if man is truly free, then God cannot exist, and conversely, if God exists, then man cannot be free. Those were the options. He said that we know for sure that we are free. We know for sure that we are moral, volitional creatures. So that proves there can't be a God.

Sartre argued that freedom means autonomy. And unless your freedom is elevated to the level of autonomy—meaning "self-law" or "self-rule"—your supposed freedom is but a mirage. Sartre said that to be truly free, we have to have autonomy, meaning that we have no accountability ultimately to anyone outside ourselves. If I am autonomous, if I rule myself, then there is no room for a sovereign omnipotent deity who reigns in heaven over all things.

If you want to find an insoluble contradiction, an antinomy that no amount of insight can resolve, it would be the conflict between divine sovereignty and human autonomy. Those two cannot mutually exist in the same universe, just as an immovable object and an irresistible force cannot exist in the same universe. We can conceive of a force that is irresistible, and we can conceive of an object that is immovable. What reason cannot conceive is the coexistence of two objects, one of which is immovable and the other of which is irresistible. Why not? If an irresistible force meets an immovable object and the object moves, what does that tell you about the object? It's not immovable. If an irresistible force meets an immovable object and it doesn't move, what does that tell you about the irresistible force? It wasn't irresistible.

What you can't have is a universe with a sovereign God and an autonomous creature. But only if you think of human freedom as rising to the level of autonomy do you have this problem. The Bible does not teach that human beings have been given autonomy by God. On the contrary, autonomy is the illegitimate, illicit reach of creatures made in submission to a sovereign God. When God put Adam and Eve in the garden, He did not tell them that they were not allowed to do anything. He did not tell them they could not avail themselves of any of the trees and their beautiful fruit. He did not tell them not to touch any of those trees or they would die. That is what the devil said God said, but that's not what God said.

In the garden, we see the introduction of the biblical concept of freedom: "Of all the trees in the garden, you may freely eat, except this one over here. You may not eat of that. If you do, you die." What God gave human beings in creation was the ability to make choices, but that ability was not unlimited. It was limited. The truth is that God is free and His creatures are free, but God is more free than His creatures are.

You would think this would be simple, but people make statements such as "God's sovereignty is limited by human freedom." That is not good theology; that is blasphemy. If God's sovereignty is limited by our freedom, then who is sovereign? We are. We then have freedom that exceeds the freedom of God Himself.

Another statement we hear is "God saves as many people as He possibly can." He would like to save everybody. He does the best He can, but if He would try to change your heart without your permission, then He would be violating your freedom, and so God can't save you unless you want to be saved. On the road to Damascus, Saul of Tarsus did not ask Christ to save him. When God intruded into my life through His sovereign good pleasure and changed the disposition of my heart, I wasn't seeking Him. I didn't ask Him to come in. He came. That's how He came to you. He didn't destroy my freedom. He elevated it, because until He did that, I was a slave to my own wicked inclinations.

When we talk about the doctrine of providence, we also talk about the doctrine of concurrence; there can be the choices of God at the same time that there are choices of men, and God works through the choices of human beings without annihilating those choices. God did not rob Joseph's brothers of their freedom. Joseph's brothers did exactly what Joseph's brothers wanted to do. God didn't coerce them, but God exercised His sovereignty through their free decisions. That's an amazing thing. It is a good thing, and I rejoice that my freedom never places a limit on God. If I choose to raise my hand as an exercise of volition, my mind has decided it would be a good thing for me to raise my hand, and that notion is communicated to the body, and I raise my hand. What if God didn't want me to raise my hand? What if God sovereignly decreed that I would not be able to raise my hand? Could He remove my ability? Yes.

The Westminster Confession of Faith says, "God from all eternity did, by the most wise and holy counsel of His own will, freely, and unchangeably ordain whatsoever comes to pass: yet so, as thereby neither is God the author of sin, nor is violence offered to the will of the creatures, nor is the liberty or contingency of second causes taken away, but rather established" (3.1). My ability to raise my hand is a real power. I can exercise real causal power by deciding I want this effect of raising my hand, but always and everywhere I live and move and have my being in God, and I can't even raise my hand without the primary power of God.

Free will does not mean autonomy; nor does it mean that as a creature you have the ability to incline yourself either to the good or to the bad with equal power. God says that by nature in your sin you're a slave. You still have a will, you still have the ability to make choices, but your choices are wicked. You are morally incapable in and of yourself, until you are enabled by God the Holy Spirit, ever to choose the holy things of God.

If God said, "Here I am. Here's Jesus. Here's no Jesus. Take your pick," the humanist believes that you have equal power to choose Jesus or not to choose Jesus. But Jesus says if that option is set before you in your sin, in your corruption, in your state of spiritual death, then you will not choose Jesus because you *cannot* choose Jesus, and the reason you cannot choose Jesus is because you *will not* choose Jesus. You cannot choose what you don't want. Choice is choosing what you want the most in a given situation. Every choice you've ever made has had a motivation behind it. It's your motivation, not somebody else's. You've never once in your whole life done something that you didn't want to do.

In an old Jack Benny skit, a man with a gun came onto the stage and said, "Your money or your life." Benny paused, and the burglar repeated himself. Benny replied, "I'm thinking it over." A burglar doesn't force you to give him money; he just reduces your options to two, and he leaves you to make the decision whether you want to give him the money or whether you want to die. You will choose according to the strongest inclination that you have at the moment.

That's the way human choice operates, and God knows that. And God has the wisdom and the power to work through our desires to bring about His plan. Even if and when our desires are altogether evil, God can and does work through our evil desires to bring about His good purposes. You meant it for evil, but God meant it for good. We must remember who is sovereign and who isn't.

Chapter Five

God's Sovereignty over Evangelism

In Romans 10, the Apostle Paul gives a promise, but it's a promise with a certain condition attached to it: "But what does it say? 'The word is near you, in your mouth and in your heart' (that is, the word of faith that we proclaim); because, if you confess with your mouth that Jesus is Lord and believe in your heart that God has raised him from the dead, you will be saved" (vv. 8–9). He announces the possibility of salvation for all people, contingent upon two things: confession with the mouth and belief with the heart.

Let's remember that the biblical doctrine of justification by faith alone is not the doctrine of justification by the *profession* of faith alone. The Bible warns us again and again that people may indeed *profess* faith in Christ without *possessing* that which they profess. Our Lord Himself said, "This people honors me with their lips, but their heart is far from me" (Matt. 15:8). At the end of His Sermon on the Mount, He gave a terrifying warning that many would come to Him at the last day saying, "Lord, Lord, did we not do this in Your name, and did we not do that in Your name?" And Jesus said, "And then I will declare to them, 'I never knew you; depart from me, you workers of lawlessness'" (see Matt. 7:22–23).

Can you imagine standing before Jesus and saying to Him, "Lord, Lord," and having Him look at you and say: "Excuse Me, I don't believe I know you. What's your name? Please leave. You have no place here with Me." We need to underscore that no one has ever been saved by a profession of faith.

We work at many kinds of evangelistic techniques to bring people to a profession of faith. It's almost as if we try hard to lead people to make a profession so that we can be at ease thinking that they are in the kingdom. One of the most common techniques is the altar call, where we ask people to get up out of their seats, come forward, and make a commitment. Or they can stay in their seats and either raise their hands, sign a card, or recite the sinner's prayer. I don't think these things are inherently wrong, and certainly there is nothing wrong with encouraging people to make a profession of faith. But we must be careful to make it clear that nobody has ever gone to heaven because he or she answered an altar call, raised a hand, signed a card, or recited the sinner's prayer. All those things can be done while not possessing saving faith. When we're engaged in evangelism, we have to remember that justification is by *faith* and not merely by a *profession* of faith. Paul said we are to confess the Lord with our lips, but we must, at the same time, believe with our hearts.

Paul went on to say, "For with the heart one believes and is justified, and with the mouth one confesses and is saved. For the Scripture says, 'Everyone who believes in him will not be put to shame.' For there is no distinction between Jew and Greek; for the same Lord is Lord of all, bestowing his riches on all who call on him. For 'everyone who calls on the name of the Lord'"—that is, who calls on Him in faith—"'will be saved'" (Rom. 10:10–13).

John 3:16 teaches us that "God so loved the world, that he gave his only Son, that whoever believes in him should not perish but have eternal life." I've heard this verse used as a proof text against the doctrines of election and divine sovereignty. But John 3:16 tells us explicitly that all who do *A* will not receive *B* (that is, condemnation), but will receive *C*. It tells us nothing about who can believe or who does believe. It only teaches us that whoever does believe will have a certain consequence from that faith, and we can tell anyone that if he puts his trust in Christ alone, he most certainly will be saved, and whosoever believes in Him will not perish. But the question is, Who can or will believe and give their hearts to Christ?

Many circles of evangelism assume that every person has the ability to make the choice to exercise faith in Christ. Many believe that faith precedes rebirth, that you have to believe in order to be born again, which is the exact opposite of what we have been proposing. We are convinced that no one in an unregenerate state will ever believe in Christ. That person is in a state of spiritual death and will not, in that imprisonment of the will, exercise his or her will to choose Christ.

As we saw in chapter 3, Jesus clearly taught this when

he said, "No one can come to me unless it is granted him by the Father" (John 6:65). And, "No one can come to me unless the Father who sent me draws him" (v. 44). "No one" is a universal negative proposition. "No one" states negatively something about the entire human race. Our Lord is making a statement about the universal state of moral inability of fallen persons. There's something that no one by nature can do. He says, "No one *can*." He doesn't say, "No one *may*." Jesus is making a statement about human possibility, what we are able to do or not do.

The word "unless" in John 6:44 indicates a necessary condition that has to be met before a desired effect can take place, and the desired effect is coming to Christ. Many assume that all a person has to do is choose Him. All people have to do in their state of spiritual death is overcome their bondage and make a decision to believe. But Jesus Christ said that no one can do this unless the Father draws him. The ability to come to Christ is a gift.

We see the word "unless" earlier in John when Jesus talked with Nicodemus about rebirth: "Unless one is born again he cannot see the kingdom of God. . . . Truly, truly, I say to you, unless one is born of water and the Spirit, he cannot enter the kingdom of God" (3:3, 5).

Now, how does this apply to our understanding of evangelism? When I was a new Christian, I talked about my conversion with every one of my friends from home, every one of my relatives, and with every person I met. I was on fire for evangelism. I wanted to be an evangelist, but I was the most ineffective evangelist I knew. At this time, a local church in the town where I attended college scheduled a revival and planned to bring in a visiting evangelist. I tried to persuade as many of my friends as possible to go to this evangelistic meeting.

This visiting evangelist said to me, "Get me any man alone for fifteen minutes, and I'll get you a decision for Christ." I wanted to learn what he was doing because I hadn't been able to get a decision from anyone except my girlfriend (who is now my wife). This man believed that evangelism was strictly a matter of the art of persuasion.

He was not in bad company. Perhaps the most famous evangelist of the nineteenth century was Charles Finney, who in many respects made mass evangelism an art form. Now, I have no reason to believe that Finney was a believer. In his systematic theology writings, he denied the doctrine of original sin, attacked the doctrine of justification by faith alone, and denied the substitutionary atonement offered by Jesus.

He was an unvarnished Pelagian who believed that people got to heaven by reforming their lives by the power of their own reason and will. In his mass evangelism, he perfected the techniques of convincing people that their lives could be improved and their virtues made manifest by making a decision for Jesus Christ. He is the father of evangelism techniques that are designed to get people to make a choice without being born again.

I believe that people do have to choose Jesus Christ to be saved; they do have to have faith in Jesus Christ to be saved. But I'm also convinced that they never will have faith in Jesus Christ or make an honest choice of Jesus Christ unless God the Holy Spirit first turns their hearts of stone to hearts of flesh and quickens them together with Christ by causing them to be born again. That has to happen first. The Holy Spirit has to raise us from spiritual death, and when He does, then we choose and make the decision that is real.

Because people know I am convinced of Reformed theology and in the sovereignty of God in all things, including evangelism, many have said to me, "Calvinism historically has been opposed to evangelism, and if you really believe in the doctrine of election, that undermines any impulse to engage in evangelism, because if from all eternity God has determined who will be saved and who won't be saved, why should we engage in evangelism at all?" In reality, however, throughout history Calvinists have been at the forefront of the evangelistic enterprise. Think of Jonathan Edwards and George Whitefield, both committed Calvinists in their theology.

It is true that people have struggled with how evangelism fits with the sovereignty of God. One of my favorite illustrations of the problem goes back to when I was a seminary student. I was in a seminar studying Edwards. There were eighteen of us in the class, two taking it for credit, sixteen taking it as auditors because they didn't want to take the exams from this particular professor. The professor had us students sit in a semicircle, and he asked us, "If God is sovereign and election is a matter of eternal decrees, why should we be engaged in evangelism?" I was delighted because he started at the other end of the semicircle, and certainly someone would answer the question before it came to me.

The first student said he didn't have an answer. Then the second. And I watched the dominoes start to fall one after another, and my safety zone kept shrinking until finally I was left alone.

The professor asked: "Well, Mr. Sproul, what do you think? If election is true, why should we be involved in evangelism?" I sputtered a little bit, then said, "One reason we should be involved in evangelism is because God commands us to do it."

He replied, a bit mockingly, "Yes, Mr. Sproul! What could possibly be a more insignificant reason to do evangelism than that the Lord God Almighty and the Savior of your soul should command you to do it?" I remember that story because I think I got the point.

God commands us to take the gospel to every tongue, tribe, and nation. Evangelism is not optional for the Christian; it's a mandate from the Lord. But the reason goes beyond that. One of the means God uses to bring His will to pass is evangelism. God not only ordains the ends, but He also ordains the means to those ends. Evangelism is the means that God uses and ordains to bring about the end of His sovereign will.

After Paul writes in Romans 10 that "everyone who calls on the name of the Lord will be saved" (v. 13), he asks a series of rhetorical questions. First, he asks, "How then will they call on him in whom they have not believed?" (v. 14). There is a prerequisite for calling on the Lord to save you:

you have to first believe that He is the Lord who saves. You're not going to call on a stick or a stone to save you because you know that they have no power to save you. But you don't call on a Savior in whom you do not first believe, and you do not believe unless you are first born of the Spirit to believe.

He then asks, "How are they to believe in him of whom they have never heard?" (v. 14). We don't believe that justification is by faith in nothing. Justification by faith alone is simple theological shorthand for justification by Christ alone. And the faith by which we are justified is a faith in Jesus. He was a real person, who did real things, who lived a life of perfect obedience, who took our sins on the cross, who exchanged His perfect righteousness for our sinfulness by imputation. You can't believe in that Jesus if you have never heard of Him. That's why the missionary mandate is so critical.

"How are they to hear without someone preaching?" (v. 14). Paul is giving us a list of necessary conditions. People will not call on someone if they don't believe, and they will not believe in someone of whom they've not heard, and they can't hear without a preacher, and "how are they to preach unless they are sent?" (v. 15). Preachers can't preach unless they are sent to preach, people can't hear until somebody tells them what to hear, people can't believe in something they've never heard of, and they will not call on the Lord unless they first believe. You see, all of these things are necessary ingredients to move someone to saving faith.

Then Paul says, "As it is written, 'How beautiful are the feet of those who preach the good news!'" (v. 15). He is citing the prophet Isaiah who wrote, "How beautiful upon the mountains are the feet of him who brings good news, who publishes peace" (Isa. 52:7).

What is Isaiah talking about? In the ancient world, when men of war went out to battle and the outcome of the battle was in doubt, news was delivered to the home front by messengers. Those messengers would be dispatched from the battle to return to town with the message. The message could be bad news or the message could be good news. Defeat was bad news; victory was *gospel*, good news.

Many towns had a watchtower, where a person was stationed to scan the horizon to see the approach of a messenger who would bring the news of the battle. The watchmen became so proficient that, even from a distance, they could tell by the gait of the messenger whether it was good news or bad news. If the messenger was bringing bad news, the lookout would see the survival shuffle of discouragement. But if he saw the feet kicking up dust on the side of the mountain, he knew that the messenger couldn't wait to get to the village because he was the bearer of good news. And so, Isaiah says, "How beautiful upon the mountains are the feet of him who brings good news." Keep in mind that the messenger was not responsible for the news. The messenger simply delivered the news, and yet, because the news he was delivering was so wonderful, his own feet were considered beautiful.

Paul draws on Isaiah to talk about the preacher of the gospel. Paul understood that the preacher is not the primary cause of quickening souls to salvation, but the preacher is a partner in the gathering of the elect. Just as our prayers are used by God as a means of grace to bring people to Himself, so the preaching of the Word is the means that God has ordained to redeem the elect. And so, I am involved in evangelism not simply because it is a sacred duty to which I must bow before a sovereign God, but also because it's an unspeakable privilege that God would allow me to carry this precious message in this earthly vessel.

Let's go back to the beginning of Romans, where Paul writes, "I do not want you to be unaware, brothers, that I have often intended to come to you (but thus far have been prevented), in order that I may reap some harvest among you as well as among the rest of the Gentiles. I am under obligation both to Greeks and to barbarians, both to the wise and to the foolish. So I am eager to preach the gospel to you also who are in Rome" (1:13–15).

Just like the Apostle Paul, I have a debt to pay, and it is the debt of evangelism. Every person who has tasted the sweetness of the gospel has an obligation to communicate that gospel to a dying world. Paul goes on to say: "For I am not ashamed of the gospel, for it is the power of God for salvation to everyone who believes, to the Jew first and also to the Greek. For in it the righteousness of God is revealed from faith for faith, as it is written, 'The righteous shall live by faith'" (vv. 16–17). Why was Paul not ashamed of the gospel? It's the power of God for salvation. God has not simply appointed the end; He has appointed the means, and He has chosen the foolishness of preaching as the means by which people will be saved.

When I speak with ministers at ministers' conferences, I like to tell the story of the last sermon Martin Luther ever preached. It was in the winter of 1546. He had been teaching his classes at the University of Wittenberg, when a message was dispatched to him pleading with him to return to his birthplace of Eisleben, because in that village two important dukes had become involved in a conflict that they were unable to resolve. The townspeople knew that both of them had such a high regard for Luther that perhaps if he returned and mediated this controversy, peace could be restored. And although Luther was not in the best of health, he answered the call. He went to his hometown and engaged in this mediation (which, unfortunately, was to no avail).

While he was there, he preached every night, and people from the surrounding villages flocked to the church to hear the famous Reformer preach. In February, two days before he died, Martin Luther preached his last sermon. In the sermon, Luther expressed his great fear for what was happening in Germany. He said that the light of the gospel had been recovered and was preached every Sunday morning in the churches and night after night in special services, yet the people continued to flock to churches that had relics. He questioned why they were doing this and proposed that they were looking for power in their Christian life. But, Luther said, that is not where God has put power. The power is in the gospel.

Most evangelicals today don't run to relics; they don't

try to find pieces of the cross or straw from the manger. We know that the power isn't there. But we try to find power in our programs. We try to find power in our methods. When will we ever learn that the power is in the gospel? God awakens people to Himself as the Holy Spirit generates faith in the hearts of people through the Word. The Spirit of God works in and through the Word. The power is in the gospel. And so, if you believe in the sovereign power of God and care about evangelism, you will use the power where God has put it.

We need to learn this over and over again and not be enticed by any substitute. The power of evangelism is not in a method. Methods might get you professions of faith, but the danger is that multitudes of people on this earth will think they are in a state of grace because they made a profession of faith but are still dead in their sin and trespasses because they have never been quickened by the power of the Holy Spirit or put their trust in the gospel of Jesus Christ. Let's be evangelists, but let's do God's work in God's way, putting our confidence in the power where God has put it. Our methods will come and go, but God's Word will never return to Him void.

About the Author

Dr. R.C. Sproul was founder of Ligonier Ministries, founding pastor of Saint Andrew's Chapel in Sanford, Fla., first president of Reformation Bible College, and executive editor of *Tabletalk* magazine. His radio program, *Renewing Your Mind*, is still broadcast daily on hundreds of radio stations around the world and can also be heard online. He was author of more than one hundred books, including *The Holiness of God*, *Chosen by God*, and *Everyone's a Theologian*. He was recognized throughout the world for his articulate defense of the inerrancy of Scripture and the need for God's people to stand with conviction upon His Word.

Free eBooks *by*
R.C. Sproul

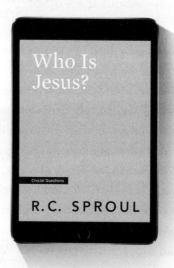

Does prayer really change things? Can I be sure I'm saved? Dr. R.C. Sproul answers these important questions, along with more than thirty others, in his Crucial Questions series. Designed for the Christian or thoughtful inquirer, these booklets can be used for personal study, small groups, and conversations with family and friends. Browse the collection and download your free digital ebooks today.

 Ligonier.org/freeCQ

Get 3 free months of *Tabletalk*

In 1977, R.C. Sproul started *Tabletalk* magazine.
Today it has become the most widely read subscriber-based monthly
devotional magazine in the world. **Try it free for 3 months.**

A Place to Find Answers

Maybe you're leading a Bible study tomorrow. Maybe you're just beginning to dig deeper. It's good to know that you can always ask Ligonier. For more than fifty years, Christians have been looking to Ligonier Ministries, the teaching fellowship of R.C. Sproul, for clear and helpful answers to biblical and theological questions. Now you can ask those questions online as they arise, confident that our team will work quickly to provide clear, concise, and trustworthy answers. The *Ask Ligonier* podcast provides another avenue for you to submit questions to some of the most trusted pastors and teachers who are serving the church today. When you have questions, just ask Ligonier.

FOR MORE INFORMATION, VISIT ASK.LIGONIER.ORG